HORROR VACUI

Horror Vacui

POEMS

Thomas Heise

Sarabande Books
LOUISVILLE, KENTUCKY

FIRST EDITION

Library of Congress Cataloging-in-Publication Data

Heise, Thomas, 1971–
    Horror vacui : poems / by Thomas Heise.– 1st ed.
        p.   cm.
    ISBN 1-932511-31-8 (acid-free paper) – ISBN 1-932511-32-6 (pbk. : acid-free paper)
    I. Title.
    PS3608.E385H67 2006
    811'.6–dc22   2005014993

13-digin ISBN 978-1-932-51131-4 (hc); ISBN 978-1-932-51132-1 (pb)

Cover image: *Prayer Book of Galeazzo Maria Sforza, 1466–1476.*

Cover and text design by Charles Casey Martin

Manufactured in Canada
This book is printed on acid-free paper.

Sarabande Books is a nonprofit literary organization.

THE KENTUCKY ARTS COUNCIL

The Kentucky Arts Council, a state agency in the Commerce Cabinet, provides operational support funding for Sarabande Books with state tax dollars and federal funding from the National Endowment for the Arts, which believes that a great nation deserves great art.

For my father, E.C.H. (d. 2001).

No farther seek his merits to disclose,
Or draw his frailties from their dread abode
(There they alike in trembling hope repose),
The bosom of his Father and his God.
—THOMAS GRAY

CONTENTS

ACKNOWLEDGMENTS

Grateful acknowledgment is made to the editors of the journals and anthologies in which the following poems have appeared or are forthcoming, sometimes in slightly different form: *Borderlands: Texas Poetry Review*; *Columbia: A Journal of Literature and Art*; *Conduit*; *The Cream City Review*; *Forklift, Ohio*; *Gulf Coast*; *Indiana Review*; *The Journal*; *Legitimate Dangers: American Poets of the New Century*; *Ploughshares*; *Skein*; *Slope*; *Southern Humanities Review*; *Verse*; *Washington Square*.

"Horror Vacui" won the 2004 *Gulf Coast* Prize in Poetry.

My gratitude to the Bread Loaf Writers' Conference and to the Millay Colony for the Arts for their support.

My deepest thanks to Christine Minas, whose support and encouragement made this book possible. I am indebted to Sarah Gorham, Jeffrey Skinner, and everyone at Sarabande for their tireless support. And many thanks to Robert Balog, John Beckman, Chris Hosea, Sabrina O. Mark, Andrew Strombeck, Alan Williamson, and Dean Young. My father: these poems are you.

I

HORROR VACUI

—you see there is nothing left to do

but gawk at the unblocked stars

and look back at our torn scrap

of black map awkwardly for a little

too long startled. You see there

is nothing left to see, which makes

the wind worse, makes we worry

the river in my palm more

until it hurts. You see, over there,

your children have taken the house

apart plank by plank and have

thrown it in the water, leaving

a yellowed grass patch as big

and blank as your absence. Your

daughter has bartered your livestock

for a golden ring. She has hung

your bathrobe in a hanging tree

and sat beneath it to weep

in the potter's field. In her eye, you

are a scarecrow on fire, you

have written your diary with a burnt

goose quill and left us to fill in

the space in the margins. You see,

your daughter of summer names you

an orange tree. In her hair, she ties

henna blossoms with a fine scarlet

thread she spins from your gloves

but it is not enough. The rain

has a home in the hollows of our

dark cloaks. I chalk my number

on a crow's wing and release him

into a mellowing year already

broken. My pockets packed

4

with dirt, I walk barefoot toward the mirror where you appear before me. Here is our elegy of twine and rotten tooth, here is a bit of hair fresh from the root of my head. I have brought you a wreath of laurel to eat at your leisure, to sit and eat in your settled melancholy. I have brought you the smell of bananas in sunlight, in my cupped hand, father, you can hear your blue macaw calling from the acorn tree. These charred acres you have created: your hermitage I will inherit in the pages of my most secret book. A train writes its way like a dotted line through the white

valley. There is ash in the air, as I go

forth in daylight, as I wade home

at evensong. The moon vibrant

as a rung bell releases birds

from my mouth. In my hand I hold

a tuning fork and clang the weather

vane, I strike my hand on the garden

wall and am returned a dull sound.

Your voice breaks through

the clouds, falls on my ear

where I leave it unbroken.

What shelter shall I assemble against

this? Could I hammer a narrow boat

from this old barn's frame. Could I

assemble an empty boat from this

old hammered frame? Could I frame

6

an empty boat for this old body's

frame? I could frame an empty body

in this old broken frame? Shall I

break an old body to fit this narrow

old frame?

II

OBITUARY [FIRST DRAFT]

Mr. William Thomas Heise, _____ ,

has finally left us from _____

[the year unknown]. Born of a spot

welder, doll maker, in northmost

[*sic*] Michigan hinterland [blue sky,

farmhouse, *don't worry, you're*

leaving]. Estranged, he was last seen

on the road in a full-white suit, white

shoes, and you're leaving [*stet stet*].

We will lead him home by horses,

skunkweed, past the poverty

of the blast furnace shining

through the trees in winter in the year

unknown sunflowers are gratefully

declined declined declined.

Burial will be at Our Lady of Holy

Mercy by the Sea where it rains

your [*sic*] incomplete.

12

EXAMINATION

Dusk I walked [*...I am here*]

under elms with my yellow stick.

[*Yes?*] I was tired of finding

I had returned once more to [*what*

was still there] a part of me I had

left broken [*broken*] and which still

depended on me [*hanging from*

an elm in wait] to speak to it [*said*

you tired. You were stranger]. And I

asked it [*when you lifted eyes up*

to branch. Said] why are the leaves

so small [*the grass fluttered*]?

And I asked it, do children make

a game of you with their sticks

[*because it hurt*] and run hiding

into forest [*when I call out*]?

And I asked should I tie a blindfold

of black cloth and knock you down

[*under our branched sky.*] as I

looked to my feet with eyes shut?

[*Said my rope has rot. Said*] And I

asked are you warm now or is your

winter coat cold [*it cannot hold us*

both. Said]? And I asked should I

leave now through the trail I made

with my pacing [*your sadness leads*

you in circles. Said]? And I asked

is it true [*no*] I am alone [*I am*

here] now? And I asked [*to take*

home,] is there a river for my

parched throat hurts [*for I am full*

of goodness. Said] from asking?

And I asked is there a spot I could

14

rest [*together*] and not talk [*I*

cannot speak. Have spoken too

much.]. So I lay down, waited [*You*

returned in circles for me] for what,

I do not know [*because the world*

is broken now, you said, you tired.]

because I thought the world no

longer answered me [*You said no*]

when I called for it [*and heard, no,*]

to leave [*and returned, yes,*

like an echo that] forever [*reverses*

itself]. I lay beside myself

[*with you.*] at last not speaking.

Hours passed into rain [*my rotten*

coat cold] in the morning, I was

alone [*under our branched sky.*

Said]. When I looked up [*you*

should have not looked] night

had blown the leaves [*because*

leaves were feathers] from the elms

and the sky bare blue [*it hurts*

to look] and the path I had paced

[*sadness*] in the tall grass was gone

[*by the wind bent back*] yet others

had opened.

16

MY PIETÀ

He held me bone-tight. He held me backward.
He held me high with the bellows
to smoke the beehive, hanging delicate
as a lung in the branches and bleeding
a half-gallon of honey while he held me. He held me
in the bathtub, scrubbed ashes from my small tongue.
He held me in the pond of his hand,
as if I were a tadpole, and wouldn't let go.
He held me hostage. I would hide
in the dumpster. Under the rain bucket
during thunderstorms. Holding my breath
among the lawn statues of gnomes and giant toadstools
until he found me, held me, walked me home.
When I fell asleep in the attic, he would carry me down
and sing to me. One winter he held a rope, lowered me
by the ankles to the well's bottom.
I ascended upside-down through the dark thermometer
with a blood orange in my teeth. He had a beard
of new snow. I held cold to his pant leg
while our dog leapt and snapped at a sound
in the air only he could hear. When I fell
in love, he reached out to me and held me down
when she slinked away on our dirt road alone,
sheepish, depressed. He held me as the constellations
mingled through the torn curtain.
A beanstalk sprouted through a hole
in our above-ground pool. A band of raccoons
commandeered the upstairs and stared
at us as he held me in his reading chair.
He grew older, he held my ear
to his artificial heart on a daily basis.

He grew sick, he held me like a suckling child.
We grew smaller and smaller and would crawl
after each other through tall grass growing through our carpet.
The walls of the house fell away.
We curled in a bird's nest. I could barely hold
his tiny thumb in my fingers.
We felt a shell growing around us.
The dog was barking.
And then rain, we could hear it tapping,
we held each other, then a blast
of hot light roared through.

PLAN B

to turn on the radio
to rearrange the scenery to gnaw on the end
of the alphabet is to soften it
I could swallow its enzymes when I'm silent
I could hammer through the windshield
and crawl onto the hood where it is warm
I've done it before
to dismantle the snowman
he is melting he is waiting for me in the cornfield
to queer the slow dance to ring in the New Year
I could sleep nude on the dryer but it would do me no good
to hold my breath
in your embrace until I buckle
when night descends on us in the open field
My life is going to change I feel it between my heartbeats
I could count to eleven when I was younger
in the old house alone
sad parrot praying *forget-me-not forget-me-not*
as if on repeat how dumb of me
I suppose I could lower the awning with a pole
close down call the afternoon a loss
so much rain I can't plan for it
so I turn up the volume to gnaw on the scenery
the sun is the color of my headache
and holding steady
I could pass out on the hood in your blue wig
it's warm I've worn it before
to welcome the snowmelt
to rearrange your embrace
to wait in the field until I feel
the bones in my black heart breaking one by one

WRECKAGE

No survivors. Nothing surfaced. No boots. No wigs.
Not your best dress. Not your nail polish.
Not my worst mood.
We lay on the bottom. Nothing could convince us.
Not the sun at thirty fathoms. Not the propellers
that cut it in two. Nor the sonar. Nor the rose garlands
they tossed us from the boat,
or the hands thrust through the clouds
of our watery sky. No one could reach us.
We lay on the bottom, talking
about nothing. Not your sister.
Not the tsunami. Not the eel that wrestled
your hair and swam off lonely.
Not your starfish
heart I broke and it grew back
crooked. Not the pattern of wreckage
scattered around us. Not the stanchion.
Not your toothbrush. Not your worst word.
Not my white sail to cover us.
There was nothing to discuss.
Nothing surfaced. Not the fuel pipe.
Not your drug use. Or your subterfuge.
My good excuse. Not the blue moon
and the minnows to swim to it.
Not the life vest. There was nothing left.
Nothing could save us.
Not your best dress. Nothing surfaced.

CORRECTIONS

We were mistaken. The Queen never loved a horse. The whole mystery will surface when we recover the missing notebook from the wreckage. "In summer, she would wander the lawn in her white robe, the light in her hair" is a misquote. Apologize. Fill in the blank with your trumpet. On page nine all the names are untrue. We were mistaken. The man running from the crime scene remains unidentified. My whereabouts: unknown. I am lost in Newfoundland. We were mistaken. Erasure on your heart's fifth amendment should read: *No*

one slept here. Memorialize it—

dream it permanent. Even

the sparrow you lifted dead

from the basket was an error.

EXAMINATION

You said yes? [*Yes.*] You said take

my body down? [*Yes.*] You said

take it down. [*Yes. Its tendons*

are stretched and tender. Said]

Yes. I know [*I want home. I know*],

because I untied it, I took it home

[*because the crows returned,*

right,] as the crows went up

from the elm's crown [*down*

the chimney, yes?] then down. Yes,

like smoke sucked backward

through broken flue: I stuttered

around the room [*Said. My body's*

soaked weight roped to your back].

White paper rain in its hair [*like*

light], torn hymn falling [*you fell*

onto your floor, right]. No, I laid it

on my bed [*Yes. You laid it on*

your bed] and asked [*to take down*

what it said] its name. [*Yes?*].

Should I speak its secret in your ear?

[*Don't*] and the body said yes?

[*please don't.*] It had a map

of black stitches on its back [*It had*

a map of black stitches on its back?]

and a mud wasp hanging in its

mouth [*Oh.*]. Its belly was smooth,

no holes [*Yes.*]. As if it never hung

from the tree [*No?*]. You'd think

god loves horses more. [*Said. I*

know god loves some horses more.]

Is the world fouled? [*It smells*

of river and eels.] Its smell seeps

24

like oil through my sleep [*Yet*]

Because [*the crows returned*]

the spirit rotted out [*with bits*

of white hymn on their wings]

or wasn't [*yet*] ever, I feel [*you*

still took it down]. When I name

its secret in your ear [*Said. Its belly*

was smooth, no holes] you'll know I

was [*in its hands,*] there and why I

came back [*from there to here*]

altered [*without a mark. Said. What*

words you couldn't take]. To find

them fouled, rotted to seed [*down,*

you wrote]? They make my breath

smell of bird [*on their wings.*]

when I speak grace. Yes. [*The body*

said yes, with its eyes it said] I

untied the secret from the tree.

Stretched, but tender. The world's

not ever [*never speak*] not stung

and lost [*its truth to me*] to me.

OBITUARY [REVISED]

Mr. William Thomas Heise, 29, entered into rest from massive heart failure on Friday, September 22nd, 2000. He was scuba diving alone at the moment of his death. Entombment will be celebrated at the Mausoleum of Flowers by the ocean. Friends welcome. His father is expected to play the organ.

ZOMBIE

In your three-piece suit and your tuxedo shoes
you're dressed as if to go, but in your coma
you do not come or go. The wife you left
has come down from the mountain to give
you a matching ring of glass. Your doll-sized
daughter has brought you a kelp flower
that smells of salt to pin to your lapel.
Into your welmish eye, she says
the world is drearful and you should go now.
But nothing rouses you from the deepwater sleep
in which you melt like an iceberg. On a canopied bier
fit for a sun king, you float and dream of what?
Your kaleidoscope? An octopus? The suitcase,
packed with a warm coat and dried apricots
for your soft teeth, waits at the door.
On the far shore your mother waves for you.
Her little white flag is a seagull's wing.
There you do not go to her. The bridge stops
in midair, the perch of the swan diver.
The canoe decays into a trough of rosemary,
so I'll bury it with roses: *He loves me, he loves*
me not, he loves me, he loves me not he loves
me not. Can you hear me? My ear to your ear
and my dumb voice boomerangs. Your brain
a beehive, its combs dormant from the first
snowfall are full of rings and echoes.
On the floor the cat crouches, lapping
your spilled coins: *clink clink clink.*
The gargoyle climbs down from his gable
to sit in your rubber plant. He sings a lullaby.
Your paper lips sip an air tube, passive

as a bored child. Your daughter has just
pulled off your caterpillar mustache.
Your wife has turned into a sunspot.
Today I have a small blue heart made of velvet.
I listen for the chanticleer to declare
all-clear for you to go. He has gone,
flown kamikaze into yesterday's sun.
Now my kingdom of dirt will not fill
the flowered urn where I will store
and sift your ruins bitter for a golden hair.
Now my arm is growing into an orange branch
as I speak. The moon has risen full
behind my leafy eyes. I want to sleep, but
the owl who is eating my tongue says no.

THESE NEW DAYS

Last night the hive in the attic
came alive, a mummified head.
The radio full of static and secret code
only a cricket could decipher.
The infinity symbol I found in the dirt
was confiscated as evidence.
A zero so large you could crawl through it.
I saw *ssshhh* trapped in a jar
of formaldehyde. I saw myself
in the startled eye of a monkey.
They came, unbolted the mirror
from my wall. Each morning,
a black mark where my face was.
They took all the locks and knobs
from the house. They took
the panes of glass, hauled them away
on their backs like a line of worker ants.
I've lived in this house a long time,
built it with my own hands. See
the way it leans when the sun shines on it.
Once in a while a dog runs past,
barking at an imaginary balloon.
The widows walk to the outskirts
to stare into The Cesspool, red at dawn.
I am more alone than a small pony.
The canary plucks out her feathers,
they grow back more yellow.
Pimpled mouse. No one is a winner.
There comes a time when the song
must be put in a cage and the cage
must be lowered by pulleys

into the river. Goodbye dandelion.
The years I was happiest. My friend
once called me Wishful Thinking.
Does a sound go on forever?
My voice deep inside your boot.
Little fish little fish little fish.

THE REMAINDER

In the country of dead pear trees, death
refuses the dog, leaves him tethered

to a stump moored in the center of the torn-up
untilled field of long grasses

shifting back and forth for hours.
A few night birds patrol

the sun's evacuation. It's weather for leaving
or being left behind. In the trees

the wind leaves its voice and moves east
without apology, as if to say *stay here*

or *dry your hands and lie down by the garden wall.*
As if the wind could sustain its intent

a little longer in your private, unchanged body,
could carry you beyond your last surviving iris.

But you've been awake for as long as you can remember
and now the fireflies failing to immolate

is all you remember. The sky is settled
in its magnitude. And the dog is howling

at what is left of his shadow lying on a stone.

THE ORCHARD OF ORANGE TREES

The orange trees were warm, what sounded like a chain saw
was in the distance, cutting a hole in the air.
It was night so the noise was louder and traveling

quickly through the leaves. My neighbor and I
were hunting in an orchard a mile from his house,
for his black labrador. Missing four nights.

Though on the third, I thought I saw him standing
in the center of the road. But then I looked again
and he was not there. Only a halo from the street lamp

and the dim repeated forms of mailboxes
before the road dead-ends with vacant fields
where teenagers throw their beer cans

before stealing in through bedroom windows.
My neighbor called the name and the sound
branched in the air surrounding us.

With a flashlight, he scanned the rows
though it only shone twenty feet or so
before the darkness washed back out of the trees.

He scanned the rows and they were long
unlit corridors. It was August and almost
five a.m. The earth was hot. And drinking

since midnight, the noise made me uneasy.
We headed toward it. Slowly,
the way you walk into a dark room

and feel for the wall. But sometimes
it isn't there. He forgot to latch the gate
and the dog escaped into the receding field

of the night. That had been four days ago.
Perhaps he fell into the river and the current pulled him
kicking through one of the culvert pipes.

Perhaps a car struck him and he lay down
moaning, an empty reverberating sound
that no one could hear. They say if they

don't reappear after three days, they never will
and I believe that. Though I saw something
in the road, it wasn't him. We had been drinking

and the oranges were wet, incandescent
like lanterns strung in the branches. They buzzed
with moths and flies, drawn there because the body

instinctively turns toward light, even when
it can kill you or destroy your eyes.
I know this because when I looked away

the air wavered like it does when you're sitting
in the dark, waiting, and you rise and walk out into a field
white with sunlight. We walked and the wind

moved through us as if our bodies were hollow.
And in the distance was a noise that made me uneasy,
though I did not say this I wanted to.

I knew the dog was dead. It had been four days;
and we were walking through a maze of trees
that kept closing behind us. Something stirred high

in the leaves, but I could not see it.
My neighbor said, *fruit bat* and *harmless*.
They swoop for insects, then turn on their wings

and sail into the air. Sometimes at night,
when they feed in the neighborhoods, they slam
into windows, and glass is not only beautiful,

it's invisible, and the body may break
but the radar passes right through. Some nights too,
the river's humid scent floods the house, and you wake up

smelling like musk, a pile of old clothes dug out
of the earth. It was August. And the ground
was hot, even after the sun sank like an orange

in a dark lake. In Florida, you never leave
your dog tied up in your backyard;
as soon as you're sewn into your cocoon of sleep,

the alligator will lumber out of the river
onto your lawn. He'll take your dog
right from the chain. This sounds unreal,

but I know it's true. On weekends, the teenagers
get drunk and haul their canoes into the river
that thins like a vein and winds through the orchard.

They bring rifles and lights. And when an alligator
surfaces, he'll look straight at them, blind,
paralyzed, unable to submerge. Some nights

rifle shots echo through the trees. I step
outside, but I do not see them. The street dead-ends
in a vacant field. The street lamps have halos

but only in the summer fog. The light flashed
into the empty rooms of the orchard and I felt
uneasy like when I stretch out my hand in the dark

and it isn't there. My neighbor kept calling
for his dog; he had disappeared and could not
hear us. On the third day I saw something,

but it wasn't him. I had been drinking.
The air smelled of musk, of leaves decaying.
The earth was full of August. We were lost

and the ground was so dark, it was like wading
through water. My legs heavy, completely immersed,
and a noise traveled over the surface.

It was only an irrigation pump in the distance,
flooding one field and draining another.
Though I did not know this, I was there,

so I can say one or two things. The alligators sink
to the bottom; and the current washes them
downstream. Though in the morning you can find

large bands of blood in the water.
And the grass turns red by noon. But it's gone
after a few days. Especially if it storms.

The weather called for rain and I welcomed it.
Lanterns hung in the branches humming
over our heads. I wanted to pull one down,

hold it in my palms, but I was exhausted,
lost in the middle of August. I thought,
lie down and forget all this. I knew

the dog was dead, but I don't know how.
We found him an hour later in a ditch in the orchard.
He was large and swollen, almost the size

of a calf and unrecognizable. That's how a body
rises after four days, but I did not say that.
My neighbor stood, shifting his flashlight.

The field draining in the distance. The morning slowly
focusing, as if gauze were being peeled
off the sky. We were slowly focusing,

as if looking at something we could not remember,

as if looking at something we did not care to remember.

IV

OBITUARY [TRANSLATED]

Mr. William Thomas Heise, 29,

wrote the remainder of the massive

stop Friday, September 22nd, 2000.

It was diving-suit only plunging

its death at the present time.

The setting with the tomb

celebrated with the Mausoleum

of the Flowers by the ocean.

Welcome friends. One expects

his / her father will play the body.

EXAMINATION

And I ask, father, how can you

depart when year's late light

[*I walked*] rends us [*back and*

forth] to other hues each darker

day? [*in our dried stalk meadow*]

And I ask, where will you go [*with*

white flowers fastened in the hair]

without your wool coat of holes I

hung [*decaying.*] from a low bough

to dry and kneeled below? [*I*

thought light formed branches

wrong.] And I ask, did you hear

the switch break from the birch?

[*And I thought wind bent*

the daylight back. Thought walk

quick to woods and not look

44

marked.] I swung the branch back

to back. As I asked, crows flew

from rye grass scared [*I*

misunderstood]. I spoke [*what*

I saw] back and forth, tongue split,

erred, prayed *why.* [*my world*

reformed. Thought the sun

a broken wheel, its rays red spokes.]

Clouds stirred trees in a whirr,

swayed a winter reed. [*Thought*

clouds were smoke, forest burned

somewhere unseen.] Without coat,

I warmed with words [*I heard*

but did not speak.] I cannot say.

[*As I walked, grass parted and shut.*

Hours came and left.] See how light

sends you forth [*I saw what god*

spoke] as days break [*in red*

and ochre. Words break] and reform

[*false. Your shadow cast a shadow*

over grass to dusk.]. My thoughts

moved shadows over grass. [*Words*

yes *and* no *echo forth*]. My back

braille, [*I kneeled to read in dark*]

do you see [*when light failed*] how

god has touched [*my eye and what*

you wrote] me with both hands

[*became illuminated.*].

THESE NEW DAYS

After the Massacre of Lost Objects
the sun went dead dark three days.
The sorrow in the orchard of orange trees
was ours, my family's. The zero fell off
the largest number in the world.
On my hand I wrote *left* and *please return
to owner.* The echo in my son's
skull was so loud we slept numb
in the living room. I walked
a mile to watch them tear off
the church bell like a pear
and throw it in the mud pit.
Sullage spilt out of the abattoir
where they were beheading
the cows with a buzz-saw
all summer. How soft the hay,
the uneaten grass. I found
my open wound and lay down
next to it in a field, my wound
the jellyfish. Each hour, halos of new colors,
phosphorescent, pulsed once, faded,
over the little earth. Little
explosions. Then a city of spires
bloomed in a full aurora
of my last hope, where, faraway,
I was waving *goodbye*, or was it *hello*,
from a future I no longer recall.

THE END OF THE IMAGINARY

They begin with so little joy knowing their stay is temporary.

They place the infant in the grass to see if it will crawl

back to them. Others walk in the garden

on the lit hill in the distance. The father

pulls a bag of dripping oranges

from the ice chest and offers one to his wife, but she's fallen

asleep to the voices of schoolchildren being chased

through the park's dark grove.

IMAGINARY SANITARIUM

To wind up here is to wander wrong,
blunder around a corner in a storm, or chased down

dragging your bent red umbrella, broken doll.
Mend in the garden on a lawn chair. With the hounds,

with the melancholy nun, her humor, your heart murmur.
She makes the rounds around you, you imagine,

wheeling her cart with a single gentian, two tiny candles,
a swallow of fluoride for your dirty mouth.

If one could lie down on the horizon, you wouldn't.
Prefer the warmth of the insular,

a room with a furnace of your own, an interior window,
an iron bed instead where you can pretend to slumber

a whole summer ruined on aspirin and prayer. Love is an old country,
now outlawed, now blue taboo. Rumors from home

slipped under the door, like runes one shouldn't read.
Often you stalk the grounds in your white gown

and insomnia. A murder of crows squawk and crack, pack
their shadows in the lemon branches.

Their wings are your black calendar. Come, count down
the moons, call them human, you will come to in another autumn.

RED GIANT, WHITE DWARF

We have given up on losing and now we find ourselves

winning again, which we hate. Strolling uptown—

all the crows make the street eerie.

I hand you a black plum

with bite marks. You drop it into your metal purse

where everything you don't want goes

until you discover you want it. This is natural,

hunting and gathering. Steam pours from a manhole,

mists the glasses I wear as part of my disguise.

In my armoire I store the perfect outfit for every occasion,

a cream suit for summers I'm in love.

You adjust my wig, call me by my secret name,

the one you hardly ever use and I thought you didn't remember.

In the park we quiet on a snowbank.

Gaze at galaxies drifting

deeper into space. Your teeth flash red

from my match's flame.

EPITAPH X

My birthright I have traded for a petal dress
and a summer eulogy. I have pawned my soul
for this opal ring, the color of a pale, taxidermied eye.

If I could carry calla lilies on my shoulder once more
like an umbrella in daylight, I would lean them
on the cemetery gate and sleep until the groundskeeper found me.

For some of us, beauty is carcinoma.
The saint's stigmata is god's rose, bestowed
for forgoing a human lover, who will, of course, die.

I died last year. My mother made her tears into crystal
earrings and clipped them to my ears. "Son, you will
pay for your sin," my father spoke from his throne of glass.

Stars burn a sharp, white nacre until they evaporate.
The moon's flamingo unfolds her iodine wings over the broken city.
My necropolis. My teeth are the fruit of your olive tree.

EXAMINATION

I am here / you said take my body

down / *said* / *stop* / *said* / the words

you breathed bitter / *hanging from*

a tree were / *I want home* / You

understand that now / I give you

myself / yes by halves / no by

switches red / *back and forth* / my

yellow stick / the wind bent the body

back / like smoke / *into my hands* / I

stood / I stood / I stuttered / *you see*

nothing / what was still there / *was I*

/ sucked backward through broken

flue / my face to earth / two red-dust

eyes opened / I could not see / *like*

light / *broken* / sends you forth

as day breaks / *parts and shuts* /

you'd think god loves / each darker

day / *under our branched sky* / I

lifted the secret up / and blew it back

out / *bitterness and beauty had*

wings / *of red and ochre* / the night

had flown from the trees / should I

speak / with a mud wasp hanging / *in*

the hand raised / with both hands /

because it hurt / yes / when year's

late light / runs hiding into forest / I

lay you on a bed of leaves / *please*

don't / touch / *my back is braille* /

is there a river / for my sadness has

broken / *it could not hold us both* /

hours passed into / my wool coat

of holes / are you cold now / should I

set you on fire / your words will

become illuminated / *I will wrap
my elms* / back and forth / with your
wet hair / did you hear / *what god
spoke* / molders to grace / *his breath
bitters the aspidistra* / decayed / he
walks the earth in circles / will lead
you / *from there to here* / altered /
and won't look back / at you /
without writing on your forehead
twice / the word *stranger* / I
cannot speak / *have spoken too much*
/ *what I could not say* / *is an echo
that reverses itself* / forever I will
take you home / *in the world* / I
found with a map of black stitches /
made with my pacing / stung and
lost / *in our dried stalk meadow* /

white flowers | the crows | drop

in the tall grass are gone |

the smoldered weight roped to my

back | is prayer | do you see | *I have*

wrapped | my hands with mourning

cloth | *because the world has broken*

| *its truth* | without sorrow | yet other

worlds opened

THE END OF TRAVEL

This time of year the lure of the impossible
is felt in the garish billboards mounted
above every street corner. Couples pushing strollers

through the mist seem full of expectation,
unfazed by weather, death, or anything worse
that might arrive unannounced, unwanted.

A few rustled papers settle in a sealed-off alleyway.
The reports say winter is delayed, stalled
offshore, unresolved; the season is nameless, shadow

and thunder. In downtown restaurants burning
with neon, people take early dinners to avoid
the untraveled commerce of intimacy.

From there, the avenues narrow to the ocean,
where the industrial boat basin is the haunt
of dockworkers after eight. The ice factory,

closed in 1938, still stands, barely, a testament
to the Age of Necessity and the sheer,
exact, miracle of ice on Sunday. And on a side street

somewhere, always, a car on fire.
Rain falling through the darker versions of ourselves
which in certain weather become almost palpable,

separate, bitter as iron broken in the mouth.
Crossing the wide-open, windy intersection
the person passing near your shoulder

may be an unknown cousin dying of cancer.
Maybe pain is genetic. Or is it seasonal?
Ahead on a side street, a worker at Tito's Garage & Tow

walks out in an apron, rubber boots,
his left hand entirely red from fishing a nail
from a paint drum earlier this afternoon,

and reads the names of the motels crowding the avenue,
The Starlite, Flamingo, The Vagabond Inn #5,
and wonders how long it will rain, wonders if he should

lock up...leave. Across the way, a youngish woman,
with a shopping bag, leans back into a building's blue facade.
A man next to her on a pay phone, talks above the tide

of the traffic about this bar or that bar, and perhaps
Richard shouldn't come, yes, perhaps not,
it's for the best. And the empty bus emerges

whale-like from the gloaming; she steps into its lit chamber
and choosing a seat directly behind the driver,
she turns to look at you, or someone who looks like you.

No amount of travel can master the calm
uneasy hours between anticipation and forgiveness.
Part of you wants to wait, part of you is waiting,

which is why the clouds moving low over the rooftops
are a sad pleasure, one which troubles. Even the maples
in the courtyard look nostalgic or Victorian, like remorse.

The stores won't reopen for thirteen hours. By then, the trees will have dried, and the newspaper lifted from the machine will feel as warm and heavy as bread in your hands.

GHAZAL FOR THE BODY

i.

Of all moments, this moment remains—you
near the window, the unmade bed, the morning light is blue as a
    museum's.

In sleep we devised a language of our own understanding,
the bridge between our bodies spanned in a shut eye.

Nothing is endless, not even winter. Not even the walled-off space
between waking and this or that failed enterprise. Look, the door to
    the lawn opens.

The garden lightens at its own pace.
Insects awaken and punish the air.

Before sleep, silently, I water plants.
My ring clicks in a finger-dish.

ii.

The novel you have forgotten unfolds like a bird
in my hands; a child's doll sags in the train seat.

In the illuminated gaze of Týn church we remembered our Catholic
names. I have heard trauma returns us to a light beyond memory.

The iron gate freezes open. The tombstones dark
with rain, and two young women walk with wet flowers.

I have remained here for a long time thinking of you.
This photo shows the fish market, scales iridescent as sliced opals.

Recall that scene in *The Unbearable Lightness of Being*:
Tomas before the gray wall: Where is your life?

iii.

What remains here, a braid of history,
a quilt spun from the hair of women?

What was it that took root in the bone like sorrow?
Was it the end of travel? Was it the houses we lost to age or the age
    we couldn't lose?

Empty yourself of longing. Sell your rings.
Turn back and away where the crows widen in a turning circle
    of hunger.

There is no conversion in the Old City. The roof is still sheet
    metal. When it's cloudy, the music still is French, melodic.
A man pours tea from a brass pot fastened on his back. No,
    the past is not past, I hear radio.

Listen. You will not find me in the rooms we shared.
I am here, in the bath, where I've drawn you this circle of water.

iv.

September is a locked-up, unrestored house. Windows blank
    with whiteness that reveals. The phone releases unanswered tension.
In late noon, through the architecture of my solitude.

The day sinks in its own forgetful attention to disorder. I forget
    to write, certain words I use, I forget to use.
As I write, wind moves over the pond, wind and its depletion.

What was true a year ago is no longer. The old destinations
    have again become the old destinations.
Occlude us. Our cold, idolatrous devotion to accuracy.

Know this: there is no season between the notice of your death
    and your death.
On the other side of sleep wait the radio and the body's inertia.

Nothing is west of your face. Nothing is west of the fever
    unlocking the frontier of your body.
Your name hesitates in my chest, my love, infectious.

ROSARY

i.

*

dear mother why begin:
no amount of exhortation will bring it back

the world has been interpreted   there is nowhere to fly to

*

the long ago never coming back now the long ago going going gone

*

moon lowered in my sternum is incandescent

*

can't we be sad for a while? resting on our sides bleeding
waiting for the heart planted in the onion field to bloom

                                    into a baby's blue eye

*

day breaks black bequeaths you a bird song

                                    that's all

ii.

*

sun rising   a white mushroom overnight

*

in this new world   a green parrot rides

on the shoulder of the quiet maid   whispering secrets
                                                    to her

*

sunday morning   room to room   barefoot soughing the carpet
wonder what I might remember next

*

the sky cornflower-blue   filled with a thousand airplanes
bringing the Annunciation
                                to the poor

*

dismantling the pause between waves of noise for a moment
for what it augurs   for where   it leaves us

*

at my feet   a silky web of mildew
                                screwdriver   footprints

iii.

*

kneeling on the side of the road   the moon
over my left shoulder

                  we lift a spare tire onto the rear axle

*

in the residue of morning
swirling leaves   menus   damp garbage squats on the sidewalk
                                  next to the

*

days later on the roof I point

                  an antenna at the city like a divining rod

*

heart shoved in a pouch of figwort

iv.

*

turning a word inside out to see what
it is lined with what it sounds like

                who it belongs to

*

tkk tkk tkk   emanates from the lonely and is always

*

ripples on the surface indicate some sort of spirit

                    or is it

*

stethoscope pressed to the earth: hooves

*

I have swallowed my bracelet   I hide a sunbeam in my mouth

*

silver capsule   the plane disappeared

                into the hole where the sun was

*

wing-shadows glide over the snowy lea

*

where are we:

                                       now

v.

*

eyes palm-pressed   compressed   poulticed   closed

                                        fall in ocean then

*

deep in the woods   horns scrape make a dry crying like cicadas' wings

*

calling

vi.

*

so I believe   my own forward boot march   my own meadow foam
   blowing

*

wind branching and gathering in folding leaves into a canopy

*

folding the hands and arms into origami into the shape
of a bird that flies up into the tree back into the shape of your hands:
                                      your open arms

*

a word planted under my tongue when ten
sprout   stems outward   whorled

*

which one would you like son?
pick the left hand
                a cricket leaps clicking into hot air

70

vii.

*

a wet spiderweb hanging from a pear branch

                                           suspend it in the window, this galaxy

*

temperature falls   the moon dissolving like a tablet

*

clouds laden with sparrows   and night rain   and wind

                                     they bring on their wings to leave

*

remember my name is sweet william

I am not sweet remember

                                 I will join you in early spring I will

*

a basket of red   plucked

             from beneath your bed

               and a cage under my other arm

EXEAT

I have walked this room, margin

to margin. This cane warm and worn

where I have leaned on it. Its grain

I've polished by rubbing backward.

This room is warm because I have

lived in it, breathed the wallpaper

peeling and maculate. This floor

I have worn walking forward

and backward. My shoes I spit on,

polish with paper. Worn my skin

where the world has rubbed it. Rub

my world where the skin has worn it.

I breathe my flowers and hang them

downward. The window I lean in

and limn the meadow. This wheat

I planted to feed you in autumn.

72

My face is warm when the wind

blows forward. Scrolls of paper flutter

above me. Parallelogram of light

on my chest is a summons. The life

in this room is in the shade

of the willow. The wheat shifts my

way then backward in shadow. This

exeat is my peeling wallpaper. I have

memorized this room, margin to

shadow. The chair in the corner faces

the window. The face in the window

is in the chair in the corner. I leave

you a ruler to measure your sorrow

and the width of the heart of your

unborn daughter. On the mattress

where I've rested and risen, I leave

my imprint for you to lie down in.

Leave you a box to fold my coats in.

My body stays warm even without

them. This floor is warm. I've walked

it forward. My cane I take, I stay my

flowers. I spit on my hands, hang

them downward. I lower my window

as the wind flows inward. I follow

the wind out to light to willow.

This willow is strong, an unbuilt

shelter. Its leaves hanging down

are not strips of paper. The meadow

is   wider   than   the   frame

of the window. I wear a nimbus

of flies as I walk the meadow.

The path through wheat curves down

to water. I have memorized my name

from willow to water. My shoes stay

74

warm after I've worn them. Hair will

grow through the soles of them.

Sunlight warms water to saffron.

Birds in the lake under my shoulder,

float to the surface, then dive under.

V

THESE NEW DAYS

My love, no one said these new days each turned corner
would hold a sight to waken wonder, even in the horror of it.

No one said the cicada's song would succumb to the shrill
of the police whistle as the night call of this middleworld.

Because my loneliness is dead, I seek sanctuary in you.
Foundling, fooled but well-born, the road carries you far

from me, but I follow through autumn into the almond dark.
Even when the sky made of milk suborns me. Even the market crowds

slant at my torn shirt. When no woman in the train station
wears your birthmark, I continue. Your father's house is embers.

As is your magic mother's urn. She percolates like a geyser
in her well of ashes. Her small dry fury is worth pennies.

For a last wish hastens your breath no closer to her stone mouth
or mine. These new days, the news is a dance of death.

My hair has grown long, as if I've died and been exhumed
from the nest of the white ant. The city's sewers are my streams,

but I swear I am sweeter than them, so do not fear.
Above the airplane hangar, the iron archer turns

with her quiver of arrows to rust. She points the way
to the future. The rumors of war are over. The war has begun.

Forever in the human soil, steeped forever in the bonemeal.
These new days, I search for clues in the soldier's stare.

The snow falls in his ragged eye where you stood hours,
watching the sunlight fade on your thumbnail.

Among the insomniacs and sleepwalkers, your face is lost.
A flag snapping taut on a mast wakes an anxious child, but not you.

Now the Museum of the Missing has been dismantled,
packed in ice in unmarked boxes. So sister, sylph, what is left?

How long ago did the merman break his conch shell on the shoal,
crawl ashore, leaving a trail of slime, and singing for miles: *and miles*

to go before I sleep, the city lovely is dark and deep, the city lovely,
dark and deep. Do you see? Do you see? The new century old

as whalebone scrimshaw. Only the terror is new, summoned
home in secret or error beyond expectation, I yet know.

Not on an angel's wings from a hibernal star, but a roaring bird
torn from a nest of rocks, on a sparkling day, I spied

through my parted curtains, dip and pivot on the horizon,
carrying fire: its arrival. What could I do with hands so small

I could not tear myself from the window? The sun deep
in my sinkhole eyes. A growing canker in the mirror reflects

less of the plangent world. These new days, where?
With a spider's patience, I waited as vines crept thorned

and tangled over the transom, digesting the wall's lumber
and my echo's chamber. Under the broken bridge, stood

wonder-hearted in your red raincoat. The rough surf spoke
of nothing but a boy's astral plunge. Spurned, star-glistened,

but a poisoned seed. I am sluggish as a bled calf each day
the street does not lead to you. My flâneur's shoes wear a zero

into the earth, the widower's roses will not renew. My thought
pursued through time's dream and heaven's flame until it stops

at an acorn. New word, new word. I put sorrow into each core
my tongue touches. I put my hand in your purse and find a termite.

Once younger than grass, we were. These new days, my shadow
in a headlight glances back red-eyed, then freezes on a slurry wall.

Out in the harbor, the statue looks after the last nightboat,
glowing over the water like a single film frame. Where does it go

with its cargo of men, ashen, pressed into the portholes?
My beloved, the old poet wrote that it means one thing

to sing your beauty. But I know it is another to augur the hereafter,
then long to shove the world back into god's awful mouth.

Hour by hour your absence exhausts me. On the rooftop, your dog
howls cold for you. Howls as steam pours from his throat,

for he boils inside. Because he loves you more than the moon,
the moon disappears. Dawn comes down through the city's smoke

and girders as a burning match. Under a rutted sun
turned backward by a helicopter's propeller. These news days,

blent on love and anger. My heart hangs in the park's katsuratree,
its one fruit. I sit beneath, birds flitting east on my eyelids,

after a shower of leaves in the grief of the afternoon
sudden on a salted wind. And wonder if returned

would you discover someone else, strange in my tattered suit?
And would you cool him with aloe, and love him into the evening's river?

Or would you bury my live heart here, near yours, and carry me up
the staircase into the towering air that washes your dark hair with fire?

THE AUTHOR

Kathryn Minas

Thomas Heise

was born in northern Michigan, but raised in southern Florida. He holds an MA in Creative Writing from the University of California at Davis and a PhD in American Literature from New York University, where he also taught as a Lecturer. His poetry and essays have appeared or are forthcoming in *Legitimate Dangers: American Poets of the New Century, Columbia: A Journal of Literature and Art, Gulf Coast, The Journal, Ploughshares, Slope, Verse, Modern Fiction Studies,* and in the *Bio-Critique* series. He has been the recipient of awards and fellowships from the University of California, New York University, the Millay Colony for the Arts, and Middlebury College's Bread Loaf Writers' Conference. In 2004, he received the *Gulf Coast* Prize for Poetry. Currently he is an Assistant Professor in the Department of English at McGill University in Montreal, Quebec, where he is writing a second book of poetry and finishing a study on twentieth-century urban American culture and literature.